THE ISTHELITIC THOUGHTS

GOURAV PALIWAL

Dear reader,

This book is dedicated to all the women around the world who have fought and continue to fight for their rights, their voices, and their place in society. This is for the women who have shattered glass ceilings, challenged stereotypes, and inspired countless others to do the same.

Women empowerment is about giving women the tools, resources, and opportunities they need to succeed and reach their full potential. It's about breaking down the barriers that have kept women from achieving equality, and creating a world where women can live, work, and lead on equal terms with men.

In these pages, you'll find stories of incredible women who have overcome adversity, challenged the status quo, and made a lasting impact on the world. These stories serve as a reminder that anything is possible when women have the support and resources they need to succeed.

So here's to all the trailblazing women of the past, present, and future. May your stories continue to inspire and empower the next generation of women to reach for the stars.

With gratitude,

Gourav Paliwal

Contents

Contents

Foreword

The Book is dedicated to all the Women and Girls who inspired the entire society in the Nation as well as the World. Those who fight for their rights and struggle to get success, we heads off to all of them and those who still struggle and not enough powerful to get their right. Then, This book inspire them and get them idea to get their soulful achievement.

PREFACE

Women have come a long way since the days of being seen as mere objects or second-class citizens. Today, women have shattered the glass ceiling, shattered the stereotypes, and taken their place as powerful and influential members of society. Despite this progress, however, there is still much work to be done to ensure that all women have the opportunities, resources, and support they need to reach their full potential.

This book is dedicated to the idea of women empowerment. It provides a comprehensive overview of the challenges that women still face, as well as the strategies, tools, and techniques that women can use to overcome these challenges and achieve their goals. Whether you are a young woman just starting out in life, a mid-career professional seeking to take your career to the next level, or an experienced leader looking to make a positive impact on the world, this book is designed to help you succeed.

Filled with inspiring stories, practical tips, and expert advice, this book will empower you to be your best self, pursue your passions, and make a difference in the world. So let's get started on your journey of self-discovery, self-improvement, and self-empowerment.

Acknowledgements

I would like to acknowledge the tremendous effort put into creating this book on women empowerment. It serves as a beacon of hope and inspiration for women everywhere, reminding them of their worth and their capacity for greatness.

Through its insightful stories and practical advice, this book empowers women to take control of their lives and to never stop pursuing their dreams. It is a powerful tool for women to use in their journey towards self-discovery and growth, and I am grateful for its existence.

This book will undoubtedly play a vital role in the ongoing fight for gender equality and will continue to inspire and empower women for generations to come. I extend my sincerest gratitude to the authors, editors, and publishers for their tireless efforts in bringing this book to life.

Prologue

In a world where women have been fighting for equality for centuries, it's imperative to understand the importance of empowering women. Women empowerment is the process of equipping women with the knowledge, skills, and confidence to take control of their lives and make their own choices. It involves removing the barriers that prevent women from reaching their full potential and giving them the tools to become active and equal members of society.

This book is a collection of stories, experiences, and advice from women who have overcome obstacles and found success in various fields. Through their narratives, we will delve into the challenges that women face, the strategies they have used to overcome them, and the impact they have made in their communities.

We hope that this book will inspire women everywhere to believe in themselves, to be their own advocates, and to strive for a world where women have equal opportunities, rights, and respect. Together, we can create a brighter future for women and future generations to come.

I

The history & Evolution of women's empowerment

Women's empowerment and the evolution of women's rights have a long and complex history that has been shaped by cultural, political, and economic forces. Here is a brief overview of some of the key events and movements that have shaped the trajectory of women's rights:

Ancient civilizations: In many ancient civilizations, including ancient Greece, ancient Rome, and ancient China, women were considered inferior to men and were often relegated to a subordinate role in society.

The Enlightenment and the First Wave of Feminism: The Enlightenment in the 18th century marked the beginning of the first wave of feminism, which lasted from the late 19th century to the early 20th century. During this time, women began to challenge the traditional norms and expectations that defined their roles and status in society. They advocated for their right to vote, own property, receive an education, and participate in the public sphere.

World War I and II and the Second Wave of Feminism: The Second World War and the social and economic changes that followed it helped to catalyze the second wave of feminism, which lasted from the 1960s to the 1980s. During this time, women demanded equal rights in the workplace, greater access to birth control and abortion, and an end to gender-based discrimination.

The Third Wave of Feminism: The third wave of feminism began in the 1990s and continues to this day. This wave is characterized by a more diverse and inclusive movement that recognizes the intersectionality of gender with other forms of oppression, such as race, class, and sexuality. Third-wave feminists have pushed for greater representation and recognition of marginalized groups, including women of color, LGBTQ+ women, and women with disabilities.

Contemporary Women's Rights Movement: The contemporary women's rights movement continues to build on the gains of previous generations, but also faces new challenges, such as the ongoing struggle for reproductive rights and the persistent pay gap between men and women. Despite these challenges, women have made significant progress in recent decades, including increased representation in politics, education, and the workplace.

These are just a few of the key events and movements that have shaped the history of women's empowerment and the evolution of women's rights. It is important to recognize and honor the efforts of the women and men who have fought for gender equality, and to continue working towards a world in which women's rights are fully respected and realized.

II

The challenges that women face in various aspects of life

Women face numerous challenges in various aspects of life, including education, employment, and political representation. Some of these challenges include:

Education

Lack of access to education: In many parts of the world, girls are still denied the right to attend school, especially in rural and poverty-stricken areas.

Gender disparities in enrollment and completion rates: Even when girls do attend school, they are often more likely to drop out early, leading to lower levels of educational attainment compared to their male peers.

Bias in the curriculum: Many countries still have gender-biased curriculums that reinforce gender stereotypes and discourage girls from pursuing certain subjects and careers.

Employment

The gender pay gap: On average, women earn less than men for the same work, and this pay gap persists across all levels of education and experience.

Unequal representation in leadership positions: Women are underrepresented in senior leadership positions and in industries such as technology and finance.

Sexual harassment and discrimination: Women are often subject to sexual harassment and discrimination in the workplace, which can limit their ability to succeed and advance.

Political representation

Underrepresentation in politics: Women are underrepresented in political office, both at the national and local levels.

Bias in the political process: Women are often subjected to gender bias and discrimination in the political arena, and their ideas and contributions are not given equal weight or attention.

Lack of support for women's issues: Political systems often do not prioritize or adequately address issues that disproportionately affect women, such as reproductive health and rights.

These are some of the major challenges that women face in education, employment, and political representation. Addressing these challenges and promoting gender equality is essential for achieving a more just and equitable society.

III

The impact of gender bias and discrimination on women

Gender bias and discrimination have a significant and far-reaching impact on women, affecting their lives in numerous ways. These issues can limit women's access to opportunities, including education, employment, and leadership positions, and can result in unequal pay and limited job advancement. This, in turn, can have a profound impact on women's financial stability and independence.

Gender bias and discrimination can also have negative effects on women's mental and physical health. Women who experience discrimination may feel isolated, marginalized, and devalued, which can lead to low self-esteem, depression, and other mental health problems. Additionally, women who face gender bias in the workplace may experience increased stress and anxiety, leading to physical health problems such as headaches, sleep disturbances, and heart disease.

Combatting gender bias and discrimination is essential to promoting gender equality and creating a more just and equitable society. This can be done through education and awareness-raising, as well as through policies and legislation that prohibit discrimination and promote equal opportunities for all people, regardless of gender. Employers can also play a crucial role in combating gender bias by promoting diversity and inclusivity in the workplace and by taking steps to ensure that women are treated fairly and given equal opportunities for advancement.

In conclusion, combating gender bias and discrimination is not only important for women themselves but for society as a whole. When women are given equal opportunities and are able to reach their full potential, everyone benefits. It's crucial to recognize the negative impact of these issues and to work towards creating a more equitable and just world for all people, regardless of gender.

IV

The role of laws, policies, and organizations in promoting women's empowerment and gender equality.

Laws, policies, and organizations play a crucial role in promoting women's empowerment and gender equality.

Laws serve as the foundation for promoting equality and combating discrimination. For example, laws such as the Convention on the Elimination of All Forms of

Discrimination against Women (CEDAW) and the Beijing Declaration and Platform for Action, provide a comprehensive framework for ensuring that women's rights are respected and upheld. In addition, laws that address gender-based violence, such as domestic violence acts, help to create safer environments for women.

Policies are another important tool for promoting women's empowerment and gender equality. Policies that address pay inequality, provide affordable childcare, and promote equal opportunities in education and employment can help to create a more equal society. Additionally, policies that promote women's political participation, such as quotas for women in leadership positions, can help to ensure that women's voices are heard and their perspectives are represented in decision-making processes.

Organizations also play a crucial role in promoting women's empowerment and gender equality. Non-governmental organizations (NGOs) and international organizations, such as UN Women and the World Health Organization, work to advance the rights of women and girls through advocacy, education, and the provision of services. These organizations also help to raise awareness about the challenges faced by women and girls and mobilize resources to address these challenges.

In conclusion, laws, policies, and organizations are all important tools for promoting women's empowerment and gender equality. By working together, they can create a more equal and just society where women and girls have the same opportunities and rights as men.

V
The benefits of women's empowerment.

Women's empowerment can bring a range of benefits for individuals, communities, and society as a whole. Some of these benefits include:

Increased economic growth: Women's empowerment can increase economic growth by tapping into a larger pool of human capital and promoting gender equality in the workplace. This can lead to higher productivity, better decision-making, and increased innovation.

Improved health outcomes: Women's empowerment can lead to improved health outcomes, particularly in terms of maternal and child health. Empowered women are more likely to have access to health services, information, and resources, and to be able to make informed decisions about their health.

Strengthened communities: Women's empowerment can strengthen communities by giving women a greater voice in decision-making, and by promoting gender equality. This can lead to more inclusive and responsive communities, as well as reduced violence and conflict.

Better educational outcomes: Empowered women are more likely to have access to education and to be able to make decisions about their own learning. This can lead to improved literacy rates, particularly for girls, and better educational outcomes for future generations.

Improved social and political equality: Women's empowerment can contribute to improved social and political equality, by promoting gender equality and giving women a greater voice in decision-making. This can lead to more inclusive and democratic societies, and can also help to address issues such as violence against women.

Overall, women's empowerment can have a transformative effect on individuals, communities, and society as a whole, by promoting gender equality and improving a range of outcomes in areas such as health, education, and economic growth.

VI

Success stories of women who have overcome challenges

Here are some inspiring stories of women who have overcome challenges and made a significant impact:

Malala Yousafzai - Overcame the Taliban's opposition to girls' education in Pakistan and became a global advocate for girls' education.

Ruth Bader Ginsburg - Overcame gender discrimination in the legal profession and became a Supreme Court Justice, championing women's rights and equality.

Sheryl Sandberg - Overcame the gender bias in Silicon Valley and became the first female executive at Facebook and a prominent advocate for women in leadership.

Oprah Winfrey - Overcame poverty, abuse, and discrimination to become a media mogul, philanthropist, and one of the most influential women in the world.

Arianna Huffington - Overcame criticism and resistance in the male-dominated media industry to become the co-founder of The Huffington Post and a leading voice for women in business and media.

Indira Gandhi - Overcame political opposition as India's first female Prime Minister and became a powerful leader and champion of women's rights.

Wangari Maathai - Overcame discrimination and environmental degradation in Kenya to become a Nobel Peace Prize winner and founder of the Green Belt Movement.

Ellen DeGeneres - Overcame rejection and discrimination as an openly gay comedian and talk show host, becoming a voice for the LGBTQ community and a powerful advocate for equality.

Mary Barra - Overcame the gender bias in the automotive industry and became the first female CEO of General Motors, leading the company through a major transformation.

Sojourner Truth - Overcame slavery and discrimination to become a leading abolitionist and advocate for women's rights in the 19th century

These are just a few examples of the many women who have overcome obstacles and made a lasting impact on the world. Their stories serve as an inspiration to us all and remind us of the power of determination and resilience.

VII

The importance of education, mentorship, and support networks in empowering women and promoting gender equality.

Education plays a critical role in empowering women and promoting gender equality. Education can provide women with the knowledge, skills, and confidence they need to participate fully in society, take control of their lives, and pursue their goals and aspirations. Through education, women can acquire the tools they need to challenge gender-based discrimination and to advocate for their rights and equal treatment.

Mentorship is also crucial in empowering women and promoting gender equality. Women need supportive mentors who can provide guidance, advice, and encouragement as they navigate their careers and personal lives. Mentors can serve as role models, demonstrating what is possible and helping women to overcome the challenges and obstacles they face. By providing access to networks, resources, and opportunities, mentors can help women to build their confidence, develop their skills, and advance in their careers.

Finally, support networks are essential in empowering women and promoting gender equality. Women need networks of supportive individuals who can provide them with emotional, practical, and professional support as they face the challenges and opportunities of their lives. Support networks can help women to build their resilience, expand their perspectives, and gain the courage and confidence they need to pursue their goals and aspirations. By providing a sense of community, support networks can help women to feel valued, respected, and empowered, and to overcome the isolation and loneliness that can accompany their journey.

In conclusion, education, mentorship, and support networks are key to empowering women and promoting gender equality. By providing women with the tools and resources they need to succeed, these three elements can help women to overcome the challenges they face and to achieve their full potential.

VIII

The role of men in promoting women's empowerment and gender equality and ways in which they can be allies.

Men play a crucial role in promoting women's empowerment and gender equality. They can help break down gender stereotypes, challenge gender-based violence, and promote women's leadership and representation in all spheres of life. Here are some ways in which men can be allies in this endeavor:

Educate themselves: It is important for men to educate themselves on issues related to gender equality and the impact of gender-based violence and discrimination on women.

Speak out: Men can use their platforms to speak out against gender-based violence and discrimination and to promote gender equality.

Support women's leadership: Men can support women's leadership by promoting their candidacy for leadership positions, advocating for their equal representation in decision-making bodies, and mentoring and sponsoring women's careers.

Challenge gender stereotypes: Men can challenge gender stereotypes by rejecting traditional gender roles and encouraging others to do the same.

Address gender-based violence: Men can help address gender-based violence by speaking out against it, supporting survivors, and working to change societal attitudes that condone violence against women.

Advocate for policies that promote gender equality: Men can advocate for policies that promote gender equality, such as paid parental leave, affordable childcare, and equal pay for equal work.

Lead by example: Men can lead by example in their own personal and professional lives by promoting gender equality and treating all people with respect and dignity.

By taking these steps, men can be powerful allies in promoting women's empowerment and gender equality and helping to create a more just and equitable world

IX

The impact of COVID-19 on women and the challenges faced by women during the pandemic.

The COVID-19 pandemic has had a significant impact on women across the world. Some of the key challenges faced by women during this time include:

Increased burden of caregiving: With schools and daycare centers closed, many women have had to take on the added responsibility of caring for children, elderly relatives, and other dependents. This has led to increased stress and burnout, and has made it harder for women to balance work and family responsibilities.

Job losses: The pandemic has had a disproportionate impact on industries that are heavily staffed by women, such as retail, hospitality, and care work. Many women have lost their jobs, and those who have been able to keep their jobs often face reduced hours and pay.

Economic hardship: Women are more likely to live in poverty, and the pandemic has only exacerbated this problem. Many women have faced financial difficulties as a result of job losses, reduced hours, and other economic impacts of the pandemic.

Domestic violence: The pandemic has led to a significant increase in cases of domestic violence, as people are spending more time together in close quarters. Women are disproportionately affected by domestic violence, and the pandemic has made it harder for them to escape abusive relationships.

Health risks: Women are also at increased risk of exposure to the virus, as they are more likely to work in essential jobs, such as healthcare, that put them in close contact with others.

Despite these challenges, women have also shown remarkable resilience and ingenuity in the face of the pandemic. They have continued to care for their families, adapt to new ways of working, and find creative solutions to the many problems they have faced.

X

Strategies for promoting women's empowerment and gender equality on a global scale, including through advocacy, activism, and community building.

There are several strategies that can be effective in promoting women's empowerment and gender equality on a global scale, including:

Advocacy: Advocacy involves raising awareness and influencing policy and decision-makers to address gender equality issues. This can be done through advocacy campaigns, lobbying, and media engagement to highlight the importance of women's empowerment and gender equality.

Activism: Activism involves taking action to bring about social change. This can include grassroots campaigns, protests, and other forms of direct action aimed at promoting women's rights and gender equality.

Community building: Building communities of women and allies who can support each other and work together towards gender equality is a crucial part of promoting women's empowerment. This can involve creating safe spaces for women to come together, share their experiences, and find support and mentorship.

Education and Awareness: Raising awareness about gender equality and women's rights is critical to promoting women's empowerment. This can include educating communities about the impact of gender-based violence, promoting gender equality in schools, and highlighting successful female role models in various fields.

Empowering women economically: Providing women with access to education, job training, and economic resources is crucial in empowering them and promoting gender equality. This includes initiatives such as microfinance programs, entrepreneurship training, and efforts to promote equal pay for equal work.

Legal and policy change: Addressing legal and policy barriers to women's empowerment and gender equality is critical to achieving lasting change. This can include advocating for laws that protect women's rights, working to eliminate discriminatory laws, and supporting policies that promote gender equality in the workplace and in society as a whole.

Working with men and boys: Engaging men and boys in the promotion of women's empowerment and gender equality is crucial in achieving lasting change. This can include working with men and boys to promote gender-equal norms and behaviors, and supporting their involvement in advocacy and activism efforts.

These strategies can be implemented at both the local and global level and can be tailored to specific cultural and political contexts. Effective implementation of these strategies requires collaboration and partnerships between governments, civil society organizations, and communities.

The Conclusion

In conclusion, women empowerment is essential for a balanced and just society. The Book highlights the need for equal treatment and respect for all genders, regardless of their sex. It highlights the challenges that women face in their daily lives and the importance of empowering women to achieve their full potential. The Book serves as a reminder that empowering women benefits everyone, not just women themselves. Women play a crucial role in shaping our world, and it is time to create a culture that values and supports their contributions. Women's empowerment should be a priority for everyone, regardless of gender, and we must work together to make this a reality.

By empowering women, we can break down gender barriers, improve economic and political participation, and promote equality. This can lead to greater economic growth, better health outcomes, and improved living standards for all members of society. Empowering women requires a commitment from everyone, including governments, civil society, the private sector, and individuals. By working together, we can create a world where women have the same opportunities, rights, and freedoms as men, and where everyone can thrive.

Author's Bio

Gourav Paliwal, born and raised in Saharanpur (Uttar Pradesh), is a renowned Published author known for his captivating stories and dynamic characters. With 8 years of experience in the industry, Gourav Paliwal has established himself as a leading voice in Hindi Literature. His works have received numerous awards and accolades, including the Certificates and Trophies. He also performed in the Sadhna Tv Channel, Stage performance with Kavi Sammelan & many more.

With a passion for storytelling and a deep love for language, Gourav Paliwal brings his unique perspective and vivid imagination to every page of his books. Through his writing, he invites readers on a journey through different worlds, cultures, and experiences, exploring the complexities of the human experience with sensitivity and grace.

Gourav Paliwal currently resides in Meerut, Uttar Pradesh where he continues to write and inspire readers with his works.

If you want to communicate with him or want to connect with him. Then, We provide you his Email ID and other social media handle. Go and Visit there.

Email ID - gouravpaliwal960@gmail.com

Instagram - @gouravpaliwal295